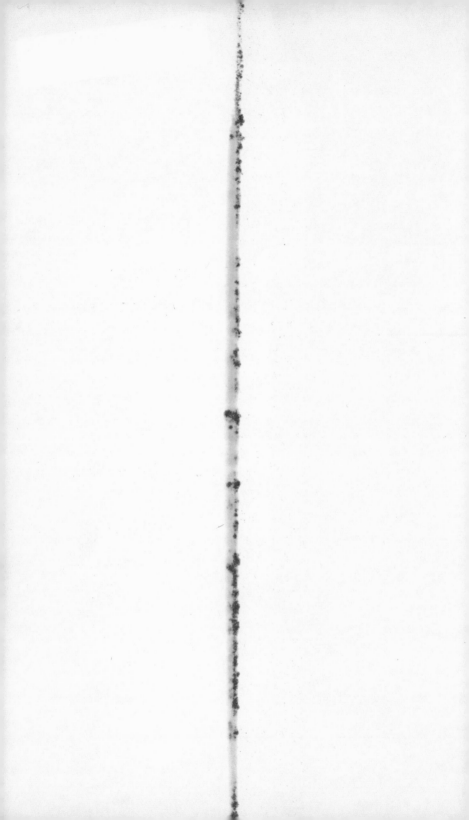

ABELARD AND HELOISE

by the same author

*

plays

THE DEATH OF SATAN
DON JUAN
THE RAPE OF LUCRETIA
STRATTON
THIS WAY TO THE TOMB

*

poetry

THE SOLITUDES
THE MONGREL AND OTHER POEMS

Abelard & Heloise

A Correspondence for the Stage
in Two Acts

RONALD DUNCAN

FABER AND FABER
24 Russell Square
London

First published in mcmlxi
by Faber and Faber Limited
24 Russell Square London WC1
Printed in Great Britain
at the Bowering Press Plymouth

The dramatic rights may be obtained
from Mary Harris Agency Ltd
81 Shaftesbury Avenue, London W1

FOR VIRGINIA

This play was first performed

at

THE ARTS THEATRE CLUB

London, November 1960

The cast was

HELOISE   Virginia Maskell

ABELARD   Iain Cuthbertson

Directed by Hugh Hunt

Settings by John Piper

Music by Thomas Eastwood

PRODUCTION NOTE

I envisage the minimum of setting: two plain tables, one each side of the proscenium at which the correspondents sit and read the letters they have written. Their movements from the desks, a question of production. They should be lit alternately. Perhaps the decor could suggest that both characters are confined. HELOISE's age should be about 26: ABELARD 45.

Mr. Thomas Eastwood has composed music for a string quartet to be played at various set places during the correspondence. A tape is available. The Score can be obtained from the composer: c/o Marjory Vosper Ltd., 53a Shaftesbury Avenue, W.1.

FOREWORD

THE following text is not a translation of the original letters written in the twelfth century between Peter Abelard and Heloise. Nor can it rank as an adaptation. It is merely a poem I wrote for the stage after having read the English translations of the letters.

The original correspondence was, of course, written in Latin and consisted of seven letters: four from Abelard, three from Heloise. I have written twelve letters here. In a few places, I have kept fairly closely to the Latin; but for the most part, I have been content to be faithful to the essence of the correspondence and have not hesitated to invent material to support it. In other places—especially in the subterfuge of Heloise's last letter—I have put dramatic needs above any other consideration.

Two texts purporting to be English translations of the correspondence exist: *The Letters of the Celebrated Abelard and Heloise*, published in Edinburgh in 1755 and translated anonymously; and *The Letters of Abelard and Heloise*, translated by C. K. Scott Montcrieff, published by Guy Chapman, London, 1925. The former is a very rare book; the latter, a limited edition of 1,000 copies and very difficult to obtain.

The eighteenth-century edition consists of six letters, including one supposedly written by Abelard to his friend Philintus, and was undoubtedly taken from the French

text of Jean de Meung. The late George Moore who
wrote a so-called historical novel on the subject, points
out in his Foreword to Mr. Montcrieff's edition that the
eighteenth-century text is a literary forgery and bears
little relation to the original Latin. Moore was probably
right: my only comment is that it is a pity we have not
more such literary forgeries. For whoever made this version was a master of English prose. I know of no better
prose than that which the forger produced in the second
and fourth Letters from Heloise to Abelard. By comparison Mr. Montcrieff's translation from the original
Latin is turgid and stiff, the style one of scholarship, and
almost as unreadable.

It seems probable to me that the eighteenth-century
translator was unaware that he was not making an accu-
rate version. I suspect that the alterations from the
original were made when the Latin was put into French.

It is not surprising that Mr. Montcrieff's version is so
poor. He had an impudent assessment of his subject and
no respect for Abelard, of whom he writes to George
Moore: 'First of all his whole affection, which seems
never to have deserved a politer name than lust, for
Heloise abruptly ceases. As her husband, he compels her
to take the veil at Argenteuil before he himself retires to
the Abbey of Saint Denis. And when, in later years, she
writes him her three immortal letters, his irritation and
boredom are manifest in every line of his replies. In his
final letter, when dealing with the use of wine in con-
vents, he actually transcribes several pages of her previous
letter to him, as though forgetting that it was she who
had written them. In his other relations also, his character
is enfeebled. True, the young prig who lectured his seniors

upon Ezekiel survives in the middle-aged prig (how curiously like certain Anglican Prelates to-day) who points out to his fellow monks of Saint Denis that their founder may not, after all, have been the Aeropagite; but the young cocksure who confuted William of Champeaux and laughed in the venerable beard of Anselm has dwindled into a querulous craven, constantly in terror of persecution, poison and the rest, magnifying his dangers with a buoyant indifference to his correspondent's natural anxiety, and piteously appealing to her for an eventual Christian burial. His once famous teaching too, has become a string of garrulous quotations, many of them singularly inept.'

With such opinions about Abelard, one wonders why Mr. Montcrieff wasted his own time mistranslating 'the querulous craven'. A great deal of literary criticism is pathological.

But none of the above is of much consequence: the combined efforts of George Moore and Scott Montcrieff cannot detract from the facts. And as I see them they are: that Heloise's letters stand beside any prose written by either sex. She was a great scholar knowing Greek, Latin and Hebrew while still in her teens; her genius lay in her capacity to feel, her talent in her ability to express those feelings. She is as articulate as Sappho or George Eliot and makes Jane Austen or Emily Brontë tongue-tied in comparison.

As for Abelard himself, it is of course ridiculous that this great poet and philosopher should be known only for his love for Heloise. It is as if Stravinsky was only to be remembered as an *émigré* to California and no-one knew that he had also been a composer.

Unfortunately Abelard's lyrics were lost. We know nothing more than 'they were sung in the streets of Paris'. But from the hymns which he composed, such as the great *O Quanta Qualia*; *Planctus*; *In Parasceve Domini*; it is impossible to avoid the conclusion that Abelard was a master of prosody even by mediaeval standards and they were very high. As a craftsman in language: Abelard ranks with Donne. I can think of few poets since who had the technical mastery to compose *O Quanta Qualia* or *Planctus*. Vivaldi and Bach achieved it in music. Schubert and Verdi had sufficient mastery but with both the age they lived in made the achievement impossible. Besides his technical ability, Abelard was an important poet in that he kept the literary influences of Greek and Roman models alive at a time when Europe had almost forgotten her progenitors and was fast sinking into a bog.

But even if he had not composed a line of poetry, Abelard deserves a niche in history. This is not the place, nor am I the person, to evaluate his great treatises *Sic et Non*, *The Christian Theology* and *Ethics*. Mr. J. Ramsey MacCallum's *Abelard's Christian Theology* (1948) makes a valuable contribution to the subject.

Briefly, it seems to me that Abelard's importance as a philosopher resides firstly in his philosophical method by his upholding of logic at a time when even the rules of reason were fast being trodden into the dogmatic marshes. He stood at the point where philosophy and religion meet. It is an important point. For him it was not sufficient to propagate religion in dogmatic terms: he asked men to look into their own nature, history and consciousness and from those data find the conclusion of Christian belief. He wanted mediaeval theology to enrich itself from its own roots, from which dogma had severed it. His contribution was to show that both Hebrew mysticism and Greek rationalism could contribute to our heritage and were influences without which Christianity was poorer. Without Abelard both Boethius and Aristotle might well have been lost. Consequent to his ignoring St. Thomas Aquinas' famous dictum: 'the truth about God, if sought by reason alone, would be forthcoming only to a few men', Abelard ran foul of Bernard. His views were before his time; and the Councils of Soissons and Sens censured him accordingly. But it is clear that the Renaissance resides firmly on this man's shoulders. It was his thought which liberated and enriched. Rome will yet have to admit him.

It might well be asked why I wrote this play which is of course so largely in terms of Abelard's relationship with Heloise when I am complaining that his reputation has been obscured because of it. The answer is that the drama has its own limitations. The stage is not the place to expound a thesis however interested you may be in it.

I was asked to write this play; I did so because Abelard has always interested me. He is one of those characters in whom emotional intensity exist alongside intellectual and spiritual vitality. I am never interested in the one without the other. There is only one kind of vitality; it has several facets. If they are not all there, I doubt if there is any there.

RONALD DUNCAN

Act One

LETTER 1

HELOISE TO ABELARD

Your hand! Your hand! The letter is in your hand.
  I thank you for it, though it is not written to me.
Of course, I recognised your handwriting,
  Of course it has not changed. The pity is that nothing
    alters;
Not even pity. And though this letter is not addressed to
  me,
  I opened it. I opened it without shame, without any
    feeling of deceit.
After so many years of silence, I do not need to justify
  what I did,
  Nor do I do that now: The letter is in your hand;
My love for that hand gives me the right, or need,
  to hold, to read what that hand had written.

  My curiosity has been punished.
How was I to guess that I should read
  my name written on every line?
Or that the whole letter was
  a brief account of our long misfortunes?
No, I had assumed, or shall I say, had feared
  That your complete silence meant
That time had given you the comfort
  It had stolen from me; that you had found
The strength to forget me, whereas I had only
  the strength not to indulge in my tender memories of
    you,

[19]

And that is not the same thing,
I have ten years of uncried tears to prove it.
  How was I to know
That you were still suffering
  as I was still suffering?
For you are a man, with qualities and intellect
  which the whole of Christendom cannot equal,
You are a man, I told myself to console myself;
  I must not expect you to feel
The emotions I was feeling. And you know how I looked
  up to you,
  Always seeing in you those qualities I lacked myself.
So I assumed that you were strong enough
  to put our suffering behind you.
There I misjudged you.
  It is not that you are weak
But that you are so strong that you can even look at your
  pain
  and need not hide from it, or pretend it is not there.

Now reading of your agony
  written in your own hand—oh Abelard, how I love
This paper, this ink that brings me
  the touch of your own hand—
All my pain which I have tried these blind years to hide
  now walks out from my heart:
It stands before me; it is as tall as I am,
  it is the same age as I am;
This pain is me.
  And since I can no longer hide it
From myself, I cannot conceal it from you
  who once possessed me wholly.

Should I be reticent and conceal
From him who once (there's pain in that word once)
   who once was so intimate with my body
He used it as his own; as I, his
   While we rode the high places of the night
And gave the day our hoofs?
   This is not, I know, how a nun should write,
My excuse for that is that she does not write it.
   There is a woman beneath each veil
And beneath this veil is, Heloise
   Who is more woman than any woman
Since it was Abelard who taught her to love.
   But though this pain is me
Not all of it is for me.
   It is for you. Nothing can ever erase from my mind
The miseries you have suffered because of your writings—
   Nothing for memory has no mercy.
And I remember how your genius was rewarded
   with only malice and envy,
How they condemned your great treatise to be burnt
   And branded you as a heretic.
   How your poems were vulgarised
By those who could not understand them.
   And finally when driven from the world
You founded this little convent which you called the
      Paraclete
   What obscene intrepretations were placed upon your
      purpose
And then, when you sought the last refuge,
   In a monastery yourself
How those whom you honoured by calling them brother
   tried to remove you from their midst

Because your presence made them aware of the mediocrity
 That was always theirs.
Your letter recounted some of this persecution
 And as I read it my tears for you broke out from my
  eyes.
Oh would that you had not written it
 for I had gained little, now all I found is lost.
Each word I read told me of the little death we died.
 All misery for those who love
Is brought to them by their eyes.
 With my eyes, I saw your grief
After my uncle had had you castrated;
 With my eyes, I saw you go
When you left me here,
 And now with the same eyes I read of your suffering:
No wonder these eyes weep.
 But I do not write to gain your sympathy
I write to you only that you might write to me.
 Be not unkind, nor deny me;
Give me that little relief that only you can give:
 A letter, this time from you to me.
Let me have a faithful account of all that concerns you
 I would know everything, however unfortunate
Perhaps by mingling my sighs with yours
 our suffering may, for each, be less?
I end this by wishing you, if you can desire it,
 (for I cannot, nor would not)
forever adieu.

LETTER 2

I wish you had not written:
  I wish your love were dead.
For if it were, then surely some of mine
  might in time die too.
That is our only hope.

  How vain and foolish men and women are
Who seek love thinking
  it is something that will comfort them;
That when found, it will give them happiness or pleasure.
  We who found it, who hold it, know differently:
Love like ours is, as you know, as I know
  The cause of all our pain.
When love is not so, it is not love,
  But mere imitation, a pretence,
An artificial rose. So do most people live
  Perhaps that is the only way they can live?
For love as we know love is too painful to be borne.
  What can its purpose be?
I sometimes wonder whether
  Love is not the birth pains of our being
For those miserable creatures like us who are trapped in
    its jaws
  have only two alternatives:
We either succumb with suffering
  Or struggle from our love of man to the love of God.
And that, that is a birth to which few men are born:

A birth I wish for
for my love is like my death.
    That is not a poetical conceit.
It is a statement of fact: for I am dead
    to everything that is not you.

You ask me to describe my condition.
    I have done that.
Though I know you mean you want to know
    Where I live? If I work? What I write?
They tell me that I am now the Abbot of St. Gildas
    And you will know that the Monastery stands on a
        cliff.
From my cell I could see the waves
    were I to look; I do look, but I do not see.
Like bulls, the powered waves lift their loins
    spending their spray on the grateful shore.
The sun rises in the East without hope
    it sets in theWest with a resignation
I cannot find. . . . Beauty bores me, Nature fails to
    distract me.

When I read, I am thinking of you;
    When I am alone, you are my meditation.
I lead the prayers; my thoughts stay by your side.
    This is my condition. Vanity made me conceal it
From the rest of the world. You have made me reveal it
    It is just that it should be to you:
Since you are the cause.

    You are my enemy, I run from.
I took my vows determined to forget you
    because I realized we could never complete our love;

[24]

Abelard to Heloise

Better, I thought for it to be severed
   than watch something so precious wither in my hand.
So I resolved to find in philosophy and religion
   the solace we could not give to each other.
I sought refuge from your love
   My discipline has been to temper my heart against you;
But I have achieved nothing.
   Distance, absence and austerity
Have only brought me closer to desire.
   Each day I swear to myself that I will forget you,
then find I cannot help but think of you;
   And am angry at my weakness
Yet grateful that I am weak.
   The paradox is that it is as if this house of chastity
Had been designed expressly to ferment my love.

You speak to me in the long hours of silence
   the solitudes and loneliness we keep, bring you to me.
I tell you, you are my enemy!
   Enemy without mercy, whose cruelty I cling to.
I hate you: I love you.
   And I pray that I may become indifferent to you
For I realize that we have nothing to hope for
   from our love. We do have something to hope for
from our religion, if we can submit our passion to it.

   How weak, wanton and foolish we are
if we cannot refine our love for each other
   into love for Him whom I believe,
And you believe, is there to support us both.
   We are by the clumsy hand of random fate
(and the hand of man) divided;

Our only union can be through Him.
Yet there you are serving two masters;
   While I am wholly given up to you:
Memory has become my mistress
   faithful as you are.

You used to call me your Master.
   You remember those hours
In which I used to fill your head
   with useless facts and questionable figures—
When you were never listening to what I was saying,
   and I was never saying what I was feeling,
And how you taught the tutor with your eyes
   and how this pupil quickly learned to conjugate your
      lips. . . .
   Those lessons cost you your innocence;
and me, my liberty; when your uncle
   (if he was your uncle
for his jealousy betrayed that his relation to you
   was something he hoped to achieve
rather than had inherited) revenged himself on me.

Oh if only I had lost the power of loving you
when I lost the ability of satisfying my love,
   then what peace, what tranquillity
The butcher would have given me!
   But the pity is, that my passion for you
grows furious by impotence.
   Though my body cannot satisfy my desires
My mind does nothing but torture me
   With memories of how you first gave yourself to me.

This is my rack,
  and the robe and habit which I wear is a masquerade.
I know this now; God has always known it:
  Though we can deceive men for a time
And ourselves for a long time
  we cannot deceive Him. I am finished.
Miserere Nobis.

LETTER 3

HELOISE TO ABELARD

I have not answered your letter
   because I could not: I have felt too miserable.
No, it was not misery: it was shame.
   For I realize that if I had not shewn you my feelings
You would not have released yours.
   You were always superior to me, especially in feeling;
I should have known that your suffering was equal; no,
     greater than mine.
   I was wrong to write to you and to ask you to write
     to me:
I am to blame.

And even now I cannot answer your letter.
For it was not a letter:
   it was a cry. When a man cries to a woman,
Be he father, brother, or lover,
   he becomes her child.
Oh what can I do to comfort you?
   My pain has moved from my heart to my breast:
I feel shame
   And I know nothing will erase that shame,
I do not ask you to forgive me:
   That would be to doubt your love.

For the last week, for seven days, your letter
Has accused me as I carried it
   where I would that I carried you.

[28]

But I had thought it better not to write again.
   I see now that would be as cruel as it would be foolish:
The damage is done, done.
   Now the only way we can solve our wounds
Is by the same means that caused them: by letters.
   It is the only way I can console you
   It is the only way you can console me.
   Let us not lose the little happiness which is left us.
Not even the world which destroyed our lives
   Can soil or spoil our letters.
I shall read that you are my husband
   And you shall see me address you as your wife.
We can be more intimate on paper,
   More tender, more gentle, of more comfort to each
     other
Than many whose happy condition
   makes them first casual, then cruel,
And finally indifferent.

   Do not therefore deny me, yourself or us.
Write, so that I may read your secret thoughts.
   I shall carry them always. I shall kiss them as I have
     kissed you.
If you can be capable of jealousy
   be jealous of the caresses I shall give your letters,
And envy only their happiness, your only rivals.
   And write carelessly without study or restraint;
I would, as a woman,
   rather hear from your heart than your brain;
I cannot live now unless I hear constantly
   that you love me, for your love
Is the element in which I live.

I am like a small bird
You are my air; blow upon me.
I am like a tiny fish,
You are my lake: flow over me.
My desert is your silence;
From your silence, I will suffocate.

Now I go to my devotions,
And I go gladly, for your sake:
it was you who placed me here,
They call me Mother,
I am:—your Mother.
You must call me wife,
I am: your wife.

LETTER 4

ABELARD TO HELOISE

It is given to few,
   to love as we love: it is given to few.
Even in my anguish, I am grateful;
   though I would be without this pain,
I cling to the cause of it.

  Absence is supposed to be the tomb of love;
And they say that people's affections
   usually die from long separation.
Then why have they not, at least, lessened our love for
    us?
   All I find from your absence
Is a constant, yet nagging remembrance of what I loved.
   I thought that if I saw you no more
You would, in time, become a memory I could recall
   at will, at will.
   But what has happened is
I have now become a memory to myself:
   You have become my identity.
And I had hoped that by fasts and studies
   You would diminish; but in spite of severe fasts,
Redoubled studies, your eyes are the only book I read.

   I confess I find this obsession tedious.
I try and do all those things I used to do before I met
   you:
   I dispute with Aristotle;

[31]

I argue commas with scholars;
    at the moment, I write a commentary on St. Paul:
but it is all utterly in vain.
And unprofitable too. For neither the Gospels nor the
    Epistles
    help a man to carry his manhood
While he is still a man. Oh why should my body
    The chalice of my soul be maimed with this dogma
      of Original Sin?

    Oh do not add to my misery
by your constancy;
    Be faithless in thought,
Since you cannot be in the body;
    Be as unlike Heloise
As I am now unlike Abelard;
    and thus wean me to indifference.
God, how I envy the happiness of those
    who have not loved as we loved.

    And what is this passion
I now write about with the enthusiasm of a schoolboy?
Is not human love, at its best;
    vain, jealous, predatory and cruel?
I am convinced it is:
    it does not deceive me.
Who has observed these brief transports before
    and watched the vicious tourney turn about and about,
till who was in, is out;
    and who was out, is in;
A tawdry roundabout
    with thighs as merchandise,
and tears to grease the ride.

Yet although I despise human love
I am not cured.
My reason condemns it,
My heart condones it.

How often have I tried, tried to denigrate you!
Listing all your faults in my mind,
recalling your failings; here, where you lied;
there, where you were unkind. . . .
Yet this has done no good at all;
Your faults are you!
I might as well extol your virtues
and remind myself of your beauty,
or ponder the mole on your neck.

I have a reputation as a Philosopher.
Some philosopher, who cannot govern his own passion!
And are you not considered one of the most accomplished
and learned ladies of the land—
I did not say, the Church?
Yet here we are both at the mercy of our emotions
Quite unable to exert our reason,
to possess the rags of our soul,
or the remnants of our sanity.

Should we not give pause
Before we hurtle down these rapids
to inevitable destruction?

Bear with me for a while while I speak like a man;
But consider this account:
Put your tears down on one side;

Add mine as well, number up our anxieties, our cares;
Compute the jealousy and grief;
  Measure the insecurity, the fear;
Then add that sum up
  And see how it weighs
by the side of love's brief pleasure!
  Fools can go bankrupt—
Why should we persist in paying
  What we can ill-afford
for something we can never receive?
  I see you yawn because I write like a grocer.
But just as I once taught you
  So now I am trying to teach myself.
It is plain to me that my future lies in my work;
  and you, to my past.
There, that frees you too. Painful?
  So is birth. But why do I now feel no relief?
No new life: A nothingness, dead—
  like stones on an untended grave.
Is it that I have no future
  and that I value all the poems I have written,
And all those I have not written,
  less than a toe on your foot?
The trouble is I am both poet and philosopher
  and the philosopher knows
That the only reality of words, is words;
  and the best of literature has not the life of a blade of
    grass.

  What then I ask myself is the purpose
Of Love like ours?
  If God has a plan, as we believe He has,

Surely then our kind of all-consuming love
  Even when and then, when it distracts from our devo-
    tions to Him
Is within His purpose too?

  What is this purpose? Is it that
I love you as an image of my own soul
  and that by loving you I will come in time to it
and to Him too?
  Are you not His emissary to me, for me
as I, in some part, for you?

  Now on these knees I pray to Him, to you,
Without shame, without profanity.
  And this is my prayer: that he gives me you,
and you lead me gently to Him;
  For I have an eternity of need;
If you take yourself from me
  You take my soul from Him.
There, I free you with one hand
  then tie you with the other.
But what is freedom?
  It is the tyranny of love.
I will write no more: for I know no more
  but this eternity of my need.

LETTER 5

I cannot tell you how your letter comforted me
    until I read the last line. That line was a knife.
You say: 'I will write no more: I know no more'
    As I read those words the paper fell from my hand.
Did you mean: you will write no more of your letter?
    Or, what I fear, that you will never write again?
I now hate your hand for writing that hurt
    Or, if it were not meant,
My hatred is for our language
    which carries such cruel ambiguities—
And in love, where there is doubt,
    We fear the wound, being so vulnerable.
If only you had written: 'I will write no more now',
    then that word 'now' would have been hallowed,
it would have been my hope: but it is not there,
    And 'no more' can mean 'never'.
That word tolls like a muffled bell;
    to-night my love feels like grief.
'Never!' It cannot be! That must not be!
    If you do not write from pity,
You must write from duty!
    Have you forgotten that you founded this Convent?
We are called your Sisters;
    We call ourselves your children;
The youngest novice here knows herself as yours.
    These walls, this chapel were built as you inspired;

This place was known once as a house for thieves;
   It was you who altered it,
Who turned it into a house of prayer.
   Can't you see you owe us your guidance?
Though this is a Convent,
   You inhabit here, for it is your fame
That has built it, your vision that gives it life,
   and it is your name that is my authority.

If you do not wish to write to me,
   I plead with you to write to us;
For you must know that though we here have taken
     holy vows
   We are not holy in ourselves:
Habits, walls and grills give us no defence, none:
   It is your duty to sustain us;
We are the vineyard you planted.
   Would you see us choked with nettles?
Virtue in us is only grafted upon our nature:
   You were the gardener,
You must know that the graft is only as secure
   As our nature: And we are women,
Any indolent man can sow a seed,
   The virtue is in the cultivation,
The diligence, the constant care and correction.
   When Paul sowed amongst the Corinthians,
Apollos watered what he had planted,
   And God gave it increase.
That ought to be the precept
   For your conduct toward us.
But why should I entreat you in the name of your
     children?

Must I use other prayer than mine to prevail upon you?
The St. Austins and Jeromes
   wrote letters to the Paulas and Melanias.
Can it be wrong for you too to imitate St. Jerome
   and discourse with me concerning the scriptures?
Or to do as St. Austin did
   and explain to me the nature of grace?
How can I teach others unless you continue to instruct
     me?
   Oh why can't men invent some instrument
In which you could speak and I could hear you
   So that distance was undone? But since they cannot
Write to me, to us.
   After all, I am your wife.
Marriage has made our correspondence lawful.
   Why will you not satisfy me in this
Since you may without scandal
   and even without offending your own vows?

   If I am in this cloister for a good reason
Persuade me to continue it with devotion.
   I need that persuasion.

Remember, if you could have forgotten,
   how I used to pass whole days
like a dog begging for morsels from your mind.
   And how when you were absent
I used to hide myself from the world in order to write
     to you.

   But this you cannot remember, for you never knew it,
how I used to contrive to see you:
   sometimes hiding your books when you were with me,

[38]

So that I could return them to you when you had gone
  pretending you had forgotten them,
And how I once feigned sickness
  only that you should see me alone in my room . . .
Yes, such contrivances, we women are forced to
  since proprieties allow us to be vehicles for passion,
but never the voice of it.

I love you: I am glad of your disability
  My uncle—(I, too, doubt that claim)
thought that I would cease to love
  Somebody who could not satisfy desire;
He measured me by the frailty of my sex:
  And thought I loved the man, and not the person.
His crime was to no purpose.
  I love you more than ever
And I will love you with all the tenderness of my soul
  to the last moment of my dying breath.
That will be my revenge on him,
  but revenge is not the reason for it.

When both the mind and the body contributed to our
    pleasure,
  I often told you I was more pleased with possessing
    your heart
And the man that you were was the thing
  I valued least about you.

  You must believe me in this:
Remembering my extreme unwillingness to marry you,
  though I knew the name of wife was honourable in the
    world
And holy in our religion,

Yet the name of mistress had greater charms for me
Because it was more free.
The bonds of matrimony
look like a contract, even when it is not needed.
I despised the name of wife
that I might live happy with that of mistress.
When the dog has no leash
we know it stays at our side from devotion;
And I needed that freedom
To prove your preference if not to you,
then to the world, and to myself.

I will write no more, beloved, to you to-day
I will write again tomorrow.
(observe how I avoid the doubt
—though you may not fear it as I)
Now I will sit alone.
Silence is eloquent
when no word can express my love.
May this silence embrace you
as I embrace it.

LETTER 6

It is not kind to remind a juggler of his dexterity
   after his hand has been cut off;
Nor tactful, to tell a painter
   how good his portraits were,
Before his eyes were put out.
   Yet so you taunt me;
When you ask me for guidance.

When you do that, you only make me realise
How completely I have lost my way.
   In the middle of my life
I am lost in a dark wood:
   I have neither eyes to see
Nor hands to feel my way.

You entreat me to write to you
   because I founded your convent.
I did not do so: it was founded by Abelard:
   he died many years ago.

And do not call me great:
   that reminds me what I am now.
What I am now is not the man you knew.
I do not deserve your respect:
   I have none for myself—
And men are like optimistic geologists
   able to find rubies and emeralds in themselves

Where there are only seams of shale or gravel.
  True, I was once called a University in myself:
When all Paris flocked to my debates at Notre Dame,
  to hear my agile and facile commentaries
on Porphyry and Boethius.
  If I seemed to know many answers then
It was because I had not met the question:
  the question of myself.
    William of Champeaux and others I defeated in argu-
      ment
Should see me now:
  devoid of logic, bereft of reason, reduced:
Now not only my manhood's gone, but the spirit's spent
  which once distinguished me.
Old Anselm would have his turn now to observe me
  grovelling on the floor of my own feelings,
Searching for the self I dropped, lost, mislaid—
  or, shall we say, betrayed?
Stuck in this posture am I the man
  to guide you?
No, leave me to search for
  the gratuity of Him in me
which I, not valuing, threw away.
  I now stand like a beggar in the gutter of my own days
After the arrogant procession of my own life has galloped
      by.

  Oh if only I had been more charitable to myself,
Merciful to myself,
  I might have some pittance left for you.

But now leave me to myself
  and do not ask me to love you;

Abelard to Heloise

That is what I am trying not to do.
    Would you thrust your holy habit
Between God and me,
    And make your present image
An unscaleable wall separating me from my devotions—
    where the memory of you alone
Has always been sufficient though unseen barrier?

Have you not had sighs and dreams enough
That you cannot afford to spend
    one little prayer of mine for Him?
Do you wish me to have ultimate peace
    or immediate tumult? On whose side are you?

I am in your hands, as a harp, I am in your hands:
    You can play upon me as you will:
It can be the silent music of tranquillity
    or the noisy chords of passion, of agony:
It is in your hands.

But if you wish for my salvation:
Withdraw from me, withdraw.
    If you love me, then shew me none!
I release you from all your tender oaths to me:
    Be His wholly:
I pray that I may lose you—
    and thus find myself in Him.

LETTER 7

HELOISE TO ABELARD

So, you wish me to withdraw!
   I will not; I will do no such thing. Even if I could,
I would do no such thing.

You ask me not to shew my love for you
   Because you see no hope for us in it;
There never is any hope for those who love:
   But I don't want hope: I want love.

Why do you write as though our emotions
   were something we could control and use?
If they were controllable they would not be emotions,
   but thoughts.
To seek a reason for our feelings
   is like seeking a reason for God.
I am as you know a poor logician
   and a worse theologian:
But I postulate this:
   that what is, in essence,
Needs no reason or justification
   other than its being.

Love is, or it is not:
   it requires no purpose nor destination:
But is, of itself; sufficient in itself
   it needs no hope, it has no cause;
And if suffering is part of love,
   then I am content to suffer.

[44]

Heloise to Abelard

The reason for your pain
    is that your pride prevents you
From submitting to your own nature
    which is part of God.
Why can you not, beloved,
    accept your love and the suffering which it is?

I suspect that you ask me to be constant
    to my devotions, and not to you,
Only because you feel guilty
    that you are the object of a passion
You do not reciprocate.
    Are you not using piety
To mask your coldness towards me?
    Will not your conscience be lightened
If I depend less on you?
    But I will do no such thing!
You say you wish to save your soul:
    Let me confess I only wish to save our love—
For a woman, that is the same thing.

If it's a sin to love
    then I am sinful and unrepentant,
Worse: grateful for my capacity to sin.
    Did you not yourself teach
In your great Treatise: '*Sic et Non*'
    that, if the soul of the world is to come to its full
        creation,
We must apprehend its reality completely?
    Did you not write
That unless evil is unique and is alone outside the Divine
        plan

[45]

Some purpose must be inherent in both good
And evil—
  both in the body and the spirit alike?

Now is the philosopher confused:
  treating me as a thing apart from my universal nature,
which is my reality,
  forgetting my love which is me, which is you.
Oh shame on you!
  What sort of God is this we worship
Who having created us wholly
  stipulates that we should be grateful
For the gift of life in part?
  Is not that God, a mad God,
If having made me woman
  He insists that I should deny my nature
As you seek to deny yours?
  I cannot learn to love Him
Unless he allow I first love you.
  Love is not divisible
For He himself is not divisible.
  Would you have me believe in a God
Who wants you to worship Him with your hands but
    not your feet,
  who wants your prayers, but not your passion?
If such a jealous God wants to take you from me
  Then I hate Him,
He is no God to me!
  I tell you, if that is the way He loves
Then I can compete with Him.
  Now hear my heresy
It is a confession without penitence:

Heloise to Abelard

I love you wholly;
And behind that word, is my hand;
    And behind that hand is my blood.

I was seventeen when you first took me to you—
—Oh where is that time fled?—
    I was a girl; your love made me a woman,
It has been a slow painful growth;
    I am grateful for the pain,
The growth I now give back to you,
    hold it in your hands like a poppy,
Learn how this woman learned to love
    And do not turn away, nor crush the petals
You yourself created.
    For this is how I love:
You, for your kindness; you, for your cruelty;
    You, for your gentleness; you, for your violence;
for the poet that you are;
    for the man that you are not,
for the child that you were,
    for the corpse you will become.
I love both your body and your mind
    Not only the chiselled sinews of your neck
but the sweat from your armpits,
    I love your vision that kindles
and your lack of vision that makes me want to take you
    by the hand.
    If this is not how God loves,
It is how I love.
    I believe we are most holy
When we become most whole.
    And if God does not love like this,

I will make love my God.
   No, I will not withdraw!

You will see that this letter has been torn across:
   Some I have written without modesty
And that will stay with me, where there is no shame.
   But that which I send here
Has, as you'll see, been written in anger
   written from jealousy
I give you the gift of my anger,
   the gift of my jealousy.
They are wings for my love
   on which I fly to you.

Abelard

O quanta qualia
  sunt illa sabbata,
  quae semper celebrat
  superna curia,
quae fessis requies,
  quae merces fortibus
cum erit omnia
  deus in omnibus.

CURTAIN

Act Two

LETTER 8

HELOISE TO ABELARD

How cruel men are
　　to teach us love
Then turn away
　　while we still . . .
How cruel you are
　　not to have written.

For three weeks I have waited—
The first week was all anticipation
　　believing each day was more certain
To bring me your letter
　　since it had not arrived the day before:
—Certainty mounting, giving disappointment further to
　　　fall.
　　The second week bruised me
Since I'd heard that you were well
　　and realized that your silence is deliberate.
At first I told myself you were being strong:
　　I lied: I knew it was not your strength
But your indifference.
You must have known how I have waited:
　　And this last week I have spent
In a fantasy since the fact was too painful to bear.

　　My fantasy has been that you were here: I have talked
　　　to you.

I have talked to you aloud:
  In my cell we have spoken softly;
In the garden we have argued, quarrelled and laughed
  And even in the chapel we have whispered
Or I have.

  Having conversed so freely with you
It seems ridiculous for me now not to commit some of
    my thoughts to paper.
  If you will not write to me;
I will write to you.
  Silence suffocates: I breathe a little
With this pen in my hand.

I am feeling resentful against you.
  Why? You shall hear.
Let every man listen to my reason:
  They teach us love, then turn away.
With what persistence did you first beg for my love!
  I surrendered soon; you took my heart without diffi-
    culty
And you abandon it with the same ease.
Now you tell me to withdraw.
  With precisely the same sophistry and persuasion
You once used to beg me to come to you,
  You now ask me to move away.
But I will not. I cannot.
  You must bear with my passion:
You made it: it belongs to you.
  You can no more disengage yourself from my heart
Than you can from your own: we belong.

Heloise to Abelard

You can atone for the misery you've caused me
By letting us be *at one*:
  By coming here so that I can see you.
—Oh! what are my eyes for?—
  And if you cannot allow yourself
To come here for my sake
  You have, as I've said, a duty
To visit this Convent for our sake.

  This is not an impossible request.
I repeat I am your wife: we are all your children here.
  I do not ask you now to give me
The comfort you once begged from me.
  That is impossible: that would be unkind.
Our vows have been made inviolate:
  Our self restraint sharpened by a knife.
All I desire is to see you
  And unless I do, it is as though my eyes were blind.
Why should I not see when I am awake
  what I visualise when they are closed?
I could show you the wall round the garden we have
    built
  from the stones which came from the stables;
I could take you into our chapel
  where we have a new statue of Our Lady
carved out of one piece of oak!
  (the model was a street urchin,
a girl with a mouth of cherries
  and a flower of innocence in her eyes);
And we could walk in our garden
  and I could show you our nectarines,
and see the juice on your lip.

[55]

But I write this without hope.
How cruel you are—
    and unnecessarily, doubling the hurt I feel,

[A pause amounting to silence]

Why should I hide the fact any more
    since you will refuse to face it:
That when I took the veil
    I did so, not out of devotion or religious zeal,
But out of my love for you.
    I vowed no more than to be yours only
And I obliged myself voluntarily to this confinement
    only because you wished to place me here.
But now if I've lost your affection
    what do I gain from my imprisonment?
I wear this habit of chastity
    and burn beneath it.
I strive hopelessly and in vain.
    Among those here who are all wedded to God,
I, alone, at their head serve a man:
    I am devoted to Abelard only.
What is more, I do not weep for my sins,
    I weep for my lover.

[A pause amounting to silence]

I recall that you made me take my vows first.
    Why was that? No, do not answer. I know the
    answer.

[A pause amounting to silence]

    I have tried, God how I've tried, to forget you
And during the tedious day
    I do succeed for a few moments;

[56]

But the nights are long and the nights are ours:
  I confess I do not lie down unless you lie beside me,
If I sleep it is only because
  I pretend my head is on your shoulder;
If I dream, I wake to tell you the dream:
  they are all of you.
And sometimes you stir,
  then I tease for a moment, then quickly surrender.
This is my condition.
  Is it wrong for me to stay here?
If you will not come to persuade me to my devotions,
  then I . . .

LETTER 9

I have written to you
  but I did not send the letters which I wrote,
And probably I shall not send this letter either.
  Our eyes are dumb;
Yet they alone speak the language of lovers
  Our lips and hands are verbose but inarticulate:
What we feel can only be expressed in silence,
  You should not have mistaken mine for indifference.

                    [A pause amounting to silence]

You plead with me to come and see you.
  The request frightens me.
You say I have a duty to you and your sisters,
  but I am suspicious of the word 'duty',
When it means inclination.
  Dearest, can you not see
That it would be impossible
  for me to play the Prior, for you to be the Abbess?
The threat is too great.
  If there were no risk,
You would have no need,
  Nor would I have that fear which reveals my desire.
We can love each other,
  I believe we can hate each other,
But indifference is something we will never achieve:
  I will not come.

                    [A pause amounting to silence]

You say I am cruel:
  I am.
I must be:
  cruelty is often a kindness we do not understand at the
    time.
                              [*A pause amounting to silence*]
Once again I urge you
  to kneel to God and not to me,
For there is no comfort in human passion:
  The only peace is in His compassion.
I love you as a man can love:
  it is not enough.
For your sake, I pray that you may return to Him
  Who is the lover
Whereas I was only a lover,
  being man—or shall we say a part?
As I write this, I see the tears you will shed
  when you read this.
But when they are dry
  read this letter over and over again:
It is the last I will ever write
  Your loving husband in Christ.
          Peter Abelard.

          [ABELARD *signs the letter, then cries out and
            throws his pen away.*]
No, tear that letter up.
  Read what I have not written.
Unread all I have written.
  My poems should not be read;
My songs should not be sung,
  They were right to burn my books.
                    [59]

For a dishonest poet is as vile
   as a false philosopher.
No, tear the letter up, I have written;
   And read this truth I have not spoken
Even to myself.
   So that my heart's been deaf
Because my soul was dumb . . .
   A volcano sealed erupts with scarlet fury:
So now my heart's fire
   spills over my soul's pasture
May only ash remain.

You asked me a question
   You say you know the answer,
But I must give you that answer:
   The pain of truth is pain
The truth of pain is truth,
   And the truth is:
That when I urged you ten years ago to take your vows
   —yes, before I took mine,
And made you dedicate your life to God,
   I did that not for your sake,
I did that not for His sake,
   —now does the lava burn . . .
The truth is, I urged you to take the veil
   only because they had destroyed my manhood,
And I, being impotent in everything but jealousy,
   Persuaded you to become a bride of Christ
Not because of your love or my love for Him
   But because I feared
That one day you might become a bride of man
   Whereas I was only part man . . .

The truth is, and it's here the sulphur scalds,
    I have betrayed my love for Him—
When you took your vows
    I knew they were for me . . .
It was to me you were being faithful.
    And when your head was shaved,
I rejoiced that no other man
    should know the beauty of your hair. . . .
I have used your holy girdle
    As a chastity belt,
And made Christ the cuckold
    Since I could not bear to be a cuckold.
The truth is:
I have not loved you
    —or only as a man can love,
And that is not enough!
    The truth is I have not loved;
The truth is I have no truth.
    Only ash remains. Adieu.

If I die here
    I will give orders
That my body shall be carried
    to the Convent of the Paraclete.
I wish you to see me in that condition
    not because I want your tears
    —then they will be too late
    —weep now to extinguish this fire that consumes me
I want you to have my corpse
    so that the horror of my carcass
May strengthen your piety:
    I shall be most eloquent then

The maggots will tell you
   What you love when you only love a man,
And I hope you will wish
   when you die to be buried beside me.
Even then I shall not be indifferent to you:
   My dusty arms will lift to embrace you.
Requiescamus in nomine Domini.

LETTER 10

HELOISE TO ABELARD

How dare you write to me like this!
   I don't know what impression you thought your letter
Would make on my mind?
   I don't suppose you even considered that
But wrote it to yourself, then had it sent to me?
   It tells me nothing I did not know,
And does nothing to relieve my present anguish;
   I had underestimated your cruelty.
I wrote to you pleading with you
   to come to see me:
Your reply is to offer me your corpse!
   You could have given me comfort
Instead you drive me into a paroxysm of grief.
   How do you think I can meditate on the elusive deity
When your contribution to my peace of mind
   Is to threaten and disturb me
With the immediate image of your own death?
   Are you so utterly naive as to believe
That your death will do anything to lessen my love for
     you?
   Do you think I do not know
That you are a man, and mortal?
   Though maggots writhe in your eyeballs
And your tongue slips from your teeth,
   I shall not feel revulsion.
What are bones or bits of hair to do with us?

[63]

Did the butcher who took away a part of you
Lessen my love for you?
   Nor will death, when it reduces you to the essence I
     adore.
On the contrary, you will be less cruel then;
   You will be more mine, then.
Does it not occur to you
   When you confess your reasons
For persuading me to take the veil
   when you knew I had no true vocation for it,
That you now have a double duty
   to live for my sake,
So that you can comfort and sustain me in my predica-
     ment?
   Of course I knew your reasons,
And I loved you for your fears.
   And if it would have given you greater security,
I would have been willing
   to have had my face scratched and clawed across.
What use had I for beauty
   once it had brought me you?
If you were to see my face now
   You would not think it beautiful:
Wild horses of anger stampede in my eyes;
   my lips are bitten, my nose red;
My brow written all over
   in your hand. Are you afraid to read
What you have written there?
   You need not, I treasure the lines:
A poem, in your own hand.
   How strange! As I write that I hear
One of the gardeners

singing in the orchard. I listen.
He is singing a song:
  a song with which he seduced his sweetheart . . .

[*Tenor solo (off)*]

    Rose of my heart,
    Hold this rose in your hand.
    It is love's flower
    Its petals bleed with my need;
    Its scent your gentleness.

    Rose of my heart,
    Hold this rose in your hand.
    Though it fades in this hour
    Our love shall be
    While there are roses till eternity.

It is just one that you wrote to me.
How often have I had to hear
  poems you wrote to me on other people's lips.
I suppose I should draw some consolation
  that though I'm no longer the object,
I was the vehicle
  that tapped your genius for others.
But it gives me small satisfaction
  to know that your words will persuade
whole armies of unborn women to enjoy
  the pleasures life has denied to me.
  I often blush now when I think
How immodest I was with you in those days:
  How I used to parade my nakedness before you
When you were trying to work,
  how I'd demand you in places where we had
little comfort, less privacy.

My excuse for all that was I was in love with the poet
Half the women of Paris were in love with too—
   I feared modesty might lose you:
And now when I need it,
   am without that quality,
And can find no reserve.
   How ill my feelings become my position;
Yet I feel no shame,
   even though I write this
beneath the silver crucifix you gave me.

Is it so strange that love should flourish
   in a house dedicated to God?
It depends on the kind of love, you say;
   but I wonder, are there different kinds of love
Or only different degrees?
   Lust, we are told, has no part in love;
but I wonder, whether or not it is an essential part
Just as remorse or penitence
   can be a prelude to a prayer?
It often occurs to me
   that God has every attribute but justice.
For when we were lustful
   and sinned whenever we could make the opportunity,
when I was your willing mistress,
   and you were my impatient lover,
how happy and childlike we were,
   but as soon as we married
Our reward was that you were castrated
   and as soon as we dedicated ourselves to God—
the result was we were tormented.
   If I have committed sins

I will not add dishonesty to them.
  My way of doing penance
For our pleasures is to recall them;
  my memory is my punishment,
if I need a punishment.
  My imagination is a torturer
who is deaf to my cries;
  And in sleep there is no refuge from you:
As I close my eyes, I open them to you;
  In my dreams, we belong;
Then I wake and walk into the nightmare
  which we call reality:
Nothing is real that is not you.
  Beloved, do I disgust you with my love?
Bear with me, if I do.
  Do not forget that though the butcher
Helped you, he did not help me.
  I am still a woman: your woman.
If God wants me to be any other,
  Why did He create me thus? I will not withdraw.
Never.

Abelard

(*as though composing, to himself*)

Vel confossus pariter
morerer feliciter
cum, quid amor faciat,
maius hoc non habeat,
et me post te vivere
mori sit assidue,
nec ad vitam anima
satis sit dimidia . . .

Close in the grave with thee I would lie
    For that is what my love would wish to do
For to live after thee would be to die
And what else is there half a soul could do?

So I would cheat
Life of its cheap deceit
Which made us one
So it could take
The whole of us from either.

To share a grave with thee
Would be like life to me.
And if we thus lie
It shall be Death not us who dies.

[68]

Abelard

Cease then my stricken lute
  Thy strings are breaking.
Would that my heart could stem
  Its bitter weeping.

LETTER 11

Dear Abelard,
      You need not feel so apprehensive;
Though you have not answered my letter,
      Nor sent me word about you,
I am not going to complain.
      I am glad that you have not written to me:
It makes it that much easier for me to tell you
      What I have found difficult to tell myself.
I do so now from the same honesty
      With which I once wrote so passionately to you.

But this is more difficult to write.
      Indeed, I have already torn this letter up twice,
And then begun again.
      The problem is:
How to be truthful and gentle—
      at the same time?
I see: it is not possible.
      Abelard, the truth is:
You have lost Heloise for ever.

      You find that hard to believe? I did too.
Indeed, I delayed writing this to you
      Until I had let time test my feelings,
And more time confirm them,
      But the truth is: I am no longer in love with you.
I read that line
      and a part of me cannot believe that I have written it

But I did write it. And it is true.
  I am no longer in love with you.
There, I have written it again!
  You are at last free from the tedium of my all-
    consuming,
all-possessive love, as I am too.
  As I am too. No more do my tethered thoughts tread
Round and round the shackle of your name.
  No more do my busy dreams shuttle across your image
To weave a cloak which worn
    revealed my nakedness.
  No longer do I wake to find my lips pressed to a pillow,
Or stand from my prayers
    to know I prayed to you.
I am free from that tyranny
    You had, or my love had made you, become.

As you will guess,
    knowing the inconstancy of my sex,
I have abandoned one lover
    Only because another has ravished me.
I am now his only
    as I was once yours completely.
Let my wantoness tell the world
    that the only constant thing about women
Is their inconstancy;
    We are incapable of faithfulness
To anything but our unfaithful natures.

But, dearest, do not be jealous
It is God alone who has taken Heloise from you.
    That is something you wished for,

This is something I strove for
  and, failing to grasp, feared I would never find.
But I have found Him.
  You will wonder how He came to possess me
Since I had remained inviolate
  So many years though betrothed to Him
dwelling in His house, wearing His ring?
  The fact is that since I last wrote to you,
I have been dangerously ill:
  the physicians feared I would die
For they knew no cure for my illness.
  You were my disease.
Since I could not have you,
  I had come to desire my death.
Four weeks, I lay without speaking,
    refusing all comfort from my sisters,
clinging to my despair
  because it was the only thing I had to cling to.
Then suddenly I woke one morning to find
  you had gone.
Another man, even more gentle than you are
  stood by my side.

He gave me his faith,
  knowing my unfaithfulness;
His eyes gentle without resentment,
  kind without reproach.
As a lover, he possesses me,
  by yielding to me.
He is passionate, without violence;
  Belonging to me, without jealousy for me.
As a father, he is fond, but not forbidding,

As a son, devoted but undemanding.
Can you wonder that I have abandoned you for Him?
    It was a miracle of mercy:
This sudden gift of grace.
    The greatness of your love
Was that you always knew that there was a love that was
        greater.
    And you tried so hard to wean me
From you to Him.
Now that I have succeeded,
Restore me to your affections:
    Assured that you are at last free of that passion
That was so destructive to us both
    Write to us occasionally.
I am re-reading Boethius and Aristotle
    and would like your comments on them.

And you need never fear a relapse from me:
    for this is true, I am no longer your mistress or your
        wife,
That is the last time I will use those words.
    I will never again think of you as my husband or my
        lover,
    and if you do not write, I will not resent it
For you are now with me always
    Since you are part of Him.

What I have done
    by finding Him, is take you into myself.
I have as it were succeeded
    In finding the you I needed within Him,
or within the self he draws out from me.
    People talk about the Love of God:

An empty phrase, a flag they wave in the air.
  But for me, it now has precise meaning
It is something as real as your hand
  And now that I hold it, or should I say, am held,
I can describe what it is that I have found.

  It is a wholeness of myself
Which is circumscribed by Him.
  But the paradox is: the circumference
Is not a limitation,
but an extension, for all is
Contained in Him.
  Like a white magnolia flower
cupped in ivory prayer,
  my tranquillity rests on the evening
And floats, still in the quiet air.
  I can now remember our misfortunes,
without regret;
  I can now be alone,
Without loneliness;
  And can sleep without dreams,
and even think of you
  without the pain of not being with you.
Abelard, you are free!
  And it is not that I love less,
but that I love more.
  I can now love as the wind loves
And be as the waves are.
  I have emerged from the chrysalis of myself,
Which was my existence,
  Into His love—
Which is now my being.

As I write this a swallow
weaves towards my window,
   I notice its restless grace:
A month ago, I would not even have seen it.
   My eyes were blind to anything that was not you.
But now, on the wings of this bird
   the whole of creation flies to me!
For the first time, I am alive
   Now that I am dead to myself:
I can be to you,
   I can be to them,
         I can even be to things.

That is what I have found.
   But even now I wonder if it's possible
that this could have happened in me.
   When we loved, as we loved,
and we find our love has gone or changed,
   We are at a loss to understand ourselves, or it.
We first doubt that we ever loved at all,
   and next question that we can again.
For love that can change
   was not love, but selflove, a need.
Needs can change, love cannot.
   But that is not what has happend to us.
We have not lost ourselves
   but found ourselves in Him.

I used to call you, beloved;
   I do so now.
But observe the word is an imperative:
   beloved, be loved; be free.

I have found another.
  I no longer need you.
It is true: You are free.

> [*She drops her pen. Her hand reaches out towards him, belying her words, showing she does not feel any of the sentiments in her letter. It is a conscious sacrifice, a gift of love to him.*]

LETTER 12

Write no more to me, Heloise;
   I beg you never write again.
Let this be the last letter between us.
   We have no longer any need
for a correspondence.
   You have found that peace
I could not give to you.
   Yet we know that a word from you,
or a word from me,
   could take away
What you might never find again.
   So let this be the last
to something that could not have an end.
   And since it is, I will write without reserve.
How happy I am that you have found that comfort
   I did not give to you
nor found myself.
   Though I confess that when I read
that you no longer loved,
   but had found someone else,
I was jealous and hurt
   as a man is jealous and hurt.
I did not guess that my rival
   was not a man, but the man.
Even so, I tried to forgive you:
   first, taking into account the condition
In which I'd placed you;
   then, remembering how I had treated you.

But in vain. It is one thing to think forgiveness,
    Another to feel it;
I failed there, utterly.
    Holding the first page of your letter in my hand,
I felt such hatred for him
    who had stolen you from me,
that I closed my eyes
    because I dared not look upon
the murder I intended.
    You once wrote that your jealousy
Was a gift of love to me;
    It is one I give now to you.
It is not easy to recognize that we are
    what we've despised: no man was ever jealous before
    me.
In those moments I realized
    my essential dishonesty.
History will probably not remember me as a philosopher
    or as a poet, but as a lover,
your lover.—
    yet I am incapable of love.
I have written and talked so much
    about love, forget all I said;
Unread all I have written.
    We know nothing about love
till we are deprived of it,
    or fear that we are,
and if we fear, we are:
    For the act of loving
does not exist in amorous play,
    In writing poems, picking flowers
or in swearing oaths, vows and promises.

Abelard to Heloise

It lies not in what we give
but in our ability to receive:
    In our trust, but we cannot trust another
if we have no truth in ourselves.
    You call me beloved,
And tell me to be loved:
    I will swim to that.

But those moments of jealousy taught me
more than I had learned from my life.
    I used to say love should not be possessive.
Should, should . . . what a word for a philosopher to use
    who's supposed to distinguish between things as they
        are,
and as he would have them—
    when convenient to him!
'Love should not be possessive', I said,
    so long as I possessed.
And even after I'd known you and loved you
    I have been unfaithful to you.
You did not know this.
    I tell you now not for your sake
but for my own.
    I was unfaithful not because I loved another
But because I loved myself.
It is now pitifully clear to me
    that whatever human love is
it is possessive.
    Perhaps God's love is too?
So write no more to me
    lest you make Him jealous
As you have made me jealous.

[79]

And be chaste in heart.
Chastity is not a restraint upon love;
    It is not a limitation,
It is a description:
    one of the measurements of love
For if we love wholly
    we do not wish to be incontinent.
When we are contained,
    we have no other need.

    Now that you have His love
you will have no need of mine.
    Beware of refusing your husband
who demands your soul,
    in preference to a lover
who does not know how to love.
    Never forget that you are now married to Christ.
Banish me from your heart entirely.
    Rest in Him whom you have found,
in Him whom I seek
    from my eternity of need.
Go beloved, go to him gaily as a bride,
    With these words, I free you
As you freed me.
    I am not jealous of Him!

> [*He thumps the desk with his fist and then his hand
> reaches out to her as her hand still reaches towards
> him. A blackout except for spots on the two hands.*]

CURTAIN

August 10th 1960